T0145283

tHE SPECIAL TWO

An Enchanting and Heart-Warming Tale of How
a Precious Boy Came into the World

SARAH KISSANE

Copyright © 2018 Sarah Kissane.

All rights reserved. No part of this book may be used or reproduced by any means, graphic, electronic, or mechanical, including photocopying, recording, taping or by any information storage retrieval system without the written permission of the author except in the case of brief quotations embodied in critical articles and reviews.

Balboa Press books may be ordered through booksellers or by contacting:

Balboa Press
A Division of Hay House
1663 Liberty Drive
Bloomington, IN 47403
www.balboapress.com.au
1 (877) 407-4847

Because of the dynamic nature of the Internet, any web addresses or links contained in this book may have changed since publication and may no longer be valid. The views expressed in this work are solely those of the author and do not necessarily reflect the views of the publisher, and the publisher hereby disclaims any responsibility for them.

Any people depicted in stock imagery provided by Getty Images are models, and such images are being used for illustrative purposes only. Certain stock imagery © Getty Images.

ISBN: 978-1-5043-1560-9 (sc)
ISBN: 978-1-5043-1561-6 (e)

Print information available on the last page.

Balboa Press rev. date: 11/07/2018

BALBOA
PRESS
A DIVISION OF HAY HOUSE

THE SPECIAL TWO

SARAH KISSANE

For Maximilian Joseph

This is a story about a magical
journey of a special little boy,
who came into the world in
the most wonderful way.

Olivia wholeheartedly wanted
to have a child of her own.
She knew if she were to wait,
it might become too late.
She often marvelled at the dark sky, amazed
at the twinkling up above her.

One night, amongst the millions
of stars shining bright, she
focused on one that gleamed
radiantly like a light.
This star was a sign, resting by the moon.
A promise from her baby that they
would meet one day soon.

She whispered her hopes to the universe,
Then waited patiently to be guided.

Sometimes it's hard to know if
you're on the right track
While you're waiting for big
dreams to manifest.
Olivia knew it could happen any day, what's
meant to be will always find a way.

To create a baby, you need an egg and a seed.
Olivia had the egg, so she set off
in search of the perfect seed
to fulfil her dream. Then she
listened to the guidance
springing from within.

Her excitement bubbled over and
she couldn't keep it in.

Help came in the form of a most
generous man who kindly gave
Olivia a magnificent seed. He
thoughtfully shared with her
the best gift of all, the start of a life she could
only imagine before.

All from a man she'd never even met.
She was full of gratitude and no regrets.
This man gave with so much love.
He was selfless, compassionate
and humble too.

From that moment on, she
knew he was the one
to help make her dream come true.

An amazing doctor handled
her with care and love,
all while Olivia watched on a screen above.

The egg and the seed so
beautifully connected,
creating her precious baby she now expected.

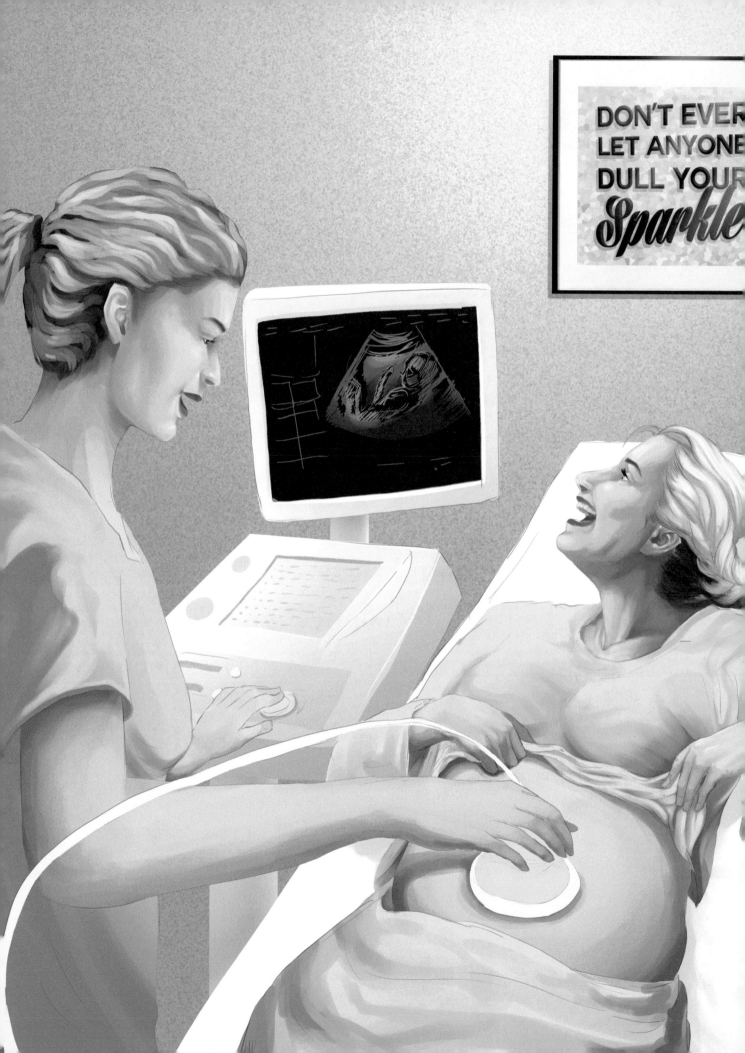

From that moment on Olivia
was delighted, and
glowed like pure sunshine,
she was so excited.
She felt wonder each time the baby danced
inside, and when she heard the precious
heartbeat she beamed with pride.

Deep inside of Olivia, the baby
began to grow, bigger
and bigger for nine months her tummy
certainly showed.

The day arrived to meet her
little miracle child.

"It's a boy!" she cried as her heart raced wild.
From that moment on, she felt complete.
Snug with her beautiful boy so sweet.

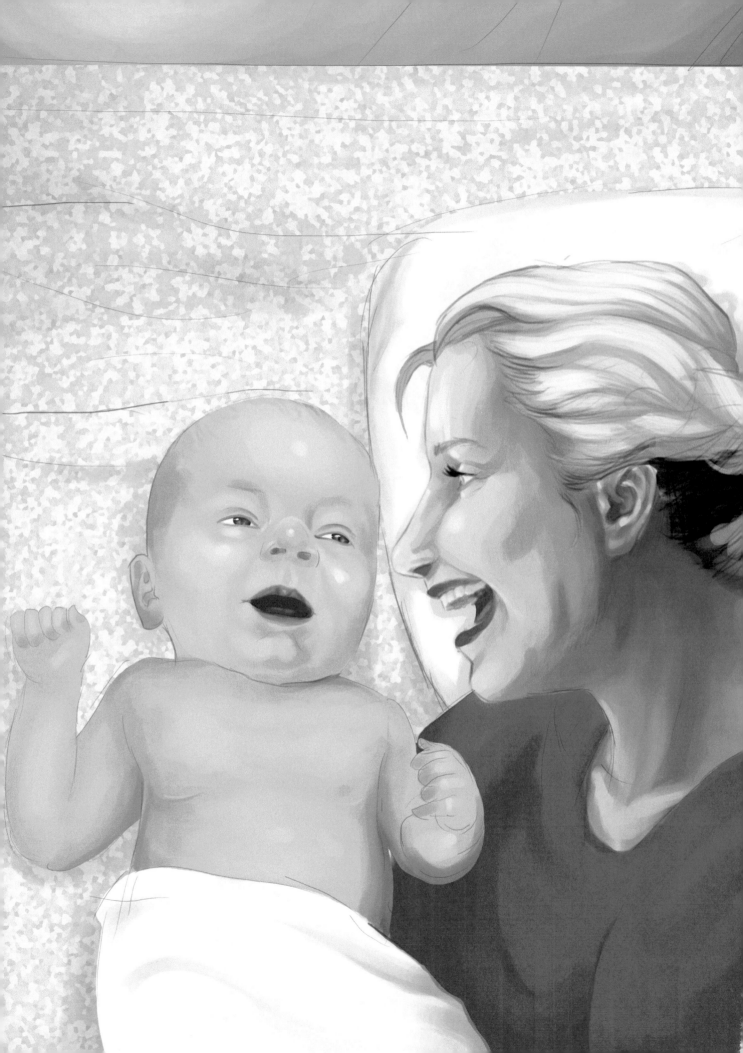

Right from the start, he
melted her heart. There
in her arms lay the most precious gift...
her gorgeous baby.

She looked into his eyes; he
smiled from ear to ear.
She whispered, "We have our very own
special family".

They laughed and cuddled,
lived life to the full.
The bond between them was unbreakable.

Their love grew stronger by
the day, as they allowed
love and light to guide their way.

Printed in the United States
By Bookmasters